The Cry For Freedom, Justice and Peace

Phineas S. Malunjwa

authorHOUSE®

AuthorHouse™ UK Ltd.
500 Avebury Boulevard
Central Milton Keynes, MK9 2BE
www.authorhouse.co.uk
Phone: 08001974150

First published by AuthorHouse   1/25/2011.

ISBN: 978-1-4567-7329-8 (sc)
ISBN: 978-1-4567-7330-4 (e)

THE TOUGHEST CHOICE

The morning was strangely quiet,
But for irregular squeaks from a chicken
Poked by another to express its might,
Since they were already scanning the yard
Picking grasses, ants, insects and worms,
As the sun peeped with the colour of gold;
And I accepted the day's challenges
With determined and unwavering spirits.

There comes a time sometime in life
When decisions must be made at once
Regardless of the dangers that lie
Along the path to freedom and justice
And that time seemed timely alive
To take the bull by the horns to survive,
I couldn't tarry for ever from the grave.

There is a time in a man's self defence,
In the defence of man's family, kith and kin,
In the defence of man's freedom and justice,
In the defence of man's domain or nation,
When brute force must be met with brute force,
Though success might seem very slim,
So that others at last may live in freedom.

It is the toughest choice I ever made
Alone, decisively, in a sober mood-
To break through the cruel enemy's net,
To walk through the wild life's habitat,
To plunge across the flowing, swelling river,
And to cross over the country's western border,
I was armed with nothing but my will power.

Thou shall not kill is God's commandment
That man can ignore at his own peril,
But God will destroy the wicked on Final Judgement
And he will save only those who do His will;

1

Therefore, the wicked should not stand aloof,
No matter the extent of their earthly power,
Even if their power appears at the roof,
The righteous, in God's name shall conquer.

He that has suffered the uttermost pain
And he that has true faith in the living God
Both have the knowledge to look up to heaven
For mercy, guidance, deliverance from God
Against the forces of evil and death
That out of avarice and lust for power
Have made themselves blind of the truth
That only the living God has all power
And the earth is God's stool in his Power.

,

MY SMALL FREE WORLD

I always yearned to go to college
To explore avenues and abyss of knowledge;
At school I read the good Old Book with zeal
I learned to read, write, do numbers and oral,
I learned about living things and non living things,
And learned arts, sciences and mathematics,
And I attained faith in the one living Almighty God
And belief in the ultimate resurrection of the dead,
And the more I learned about all the various things
The more I wanted to learn more about all things;
I was putting my feelers into the new world,
Unaware that I was driving into an ideological world,
A world, as I was to discover, full of obstacles,
And full of disenchantments, illusions and snares.

As I delved deeper into the waters of knowledge
I found myself in a dark, unpredictable deluge,
Where only the privileged class very well survive,
While everyone else pays through the nose to live,
And where money and mammon weld power
That weighs unfairly on the less privileged, the poor,
And in a world where love of another human kind
Is much less than the love of wealth and gold,
And where discrimination based on one's colour,
Ethnicity and race and religion, including gender
Is deliberately entrenched often in the law as the norm
And where the law obeys the rules of the game
And protects interests of the privileged, the powerful
Leading to economic quagmire, the ravages of misrule,
Where the greedy, the powerful manipulate the law,
And where the privileged class dwell above the law,
And enlists sycophants for snares and spies,
Wage wars and commit murder in the name of peace,
Quell dissent to protect their position in power,
And render existence of justice nothing but a misnomer.

HIGH HOPES

Below the surface of the beautiful land
Lay precious metals of various types,
Including zinc, iron, aluminium, gold,
The back bone of the country's economic engines,
In abundance, tapped and untapped,
Which colonists reaped intensely and exported.

When independence finally came
Workers, hitherto exploited, had high hopes,
But exploitation of less privileged remained the same,
Still blurred were equity and justice.
Although the oppressive regime was defeated,
The existing dilemma was still to become clearer,
Since the oppressive system expansively still existed;
Exploitation knows no race, tribe nor colour,
And most flourishes under greed driven power.

Only the rich, the elite, owned a proper mine
And paid the worker a pittance per ton of stone,
But most indigenous people lacked means to own a mine,
So polluted the land to find the precious stone;
Some squatted in search of lucrative minerals,
And others, to get the stone, ploughed river banks,
Without safety precautions, many perished in deadly pits.

THE KICKS OF A DYING HORSE

The road to independence, marred by dark and devious,
And hidden and treacherous and dangerous pitfalls,
That were, for many people, young and old, painful,
But cherished only by the greedy and the powerful
Who were armed at all times to the teeth,
By use of state machinery at will and to any length,
Without the slightest semblance of any remorse
As they crushed resistance to their greed and dominance,
Had to be traversed by all the country's genuine patriots,
Of all ages, men and women ready to brook the war's costs.

For many daunting years blacks had irksome yoke to bear
Under the reins of a cunning and brutal colonial power
Whose government instituted horrid apartheid regime
Based on deluded and ill conceived democratic system,
Where the identity of races was selfishly an underling factor
That denigrated blacks in all spheres of life for that matter
To subhuman beings, not fit to supervise white men,
Let alone head the affairs of the government or the nation,
That in the interest of kith and kin and the foreign land,
Usurped all the country's productive agricultural land,
Retarded, restricted, undermined black men's aspiration.

During the minority settler regime's reign
Upon the machinations of the imperial domain,
The destiny of the majority blacks was decided-
Disenfranchisement of the black citizenry in the land,
That defrauded freedom and equity and justice
And led to protracted war with deadly consequence.
The colonist, craftily, tenaciously held on to power,
Shamed his master and shook off the imperial power,
And stood his ground and scorned the world at large
That for many years failed his government to dislodge.

He devised new laws against all blacks' protests
And he arrested a few white men as malcontents,
And slammed black political leaders into prison

For indefinite period, in hideous, horrid dungeon;
He escorted foreign journalists out of nation's borders
And made sure they never returned as visitors.
The country fell into a deplorable open prison,
Mourned by any freedom loving democratic nation,
But they were the kicks of a dying horse,
They were signs of dawn of country's independence.

RACIAL DISCRIMINATION

Racial discrimination how pathetic, blind you are!
You are as dangerous as a venomous viper,
You ruin many people's lives, everywhere
As you eloquently spread hidden venom here and there,
In the name of your kith and kin,
In the name of your clan, tribe, race or religion
But setting them all on each other's throats,
And they wage miserable wars at terrible costs,
Each with the hope to win the war, but all in vain,
Through your evil machinations you prosper,
Your drive is avarice, desire for absolute power,
But one of the most essential elements in life
As the Bible says, "love your neighbour as you love yourself".

Racial discrimination, sordid mother of all evil!
That lays between men the base armour of ill will
To destroy the soul that calls human beings to be kind,
To pit always human kind against human kind
And to taint the social conduct of human kind
But your cohorts you cushion their fears to allay
As you conveniently set your victims at bay,
You discard your victims to their fate at will,
To roam sickly in the underworld of the caste,
While you adjust the margins of your profit
Whenever your profits begin to dwindle,
Your ways resemble the law in the animal kingdom,
But your kind will end when He gathers his children home.

THE BAD FOOD

To be told is to be denied the truth,
But vivid images pertaining to the truth,
About the horrid events of that dark night,
Still stand as testimony, without doubt,
That unarmed students fell on gun wounds
From the smoking gun that spat its lethal dose.

That reaction was uncalled for, heinous, inhuman,
And it belonged to a sphere outside due human reason,
Or it is relevant only in the natural realm of dreams
Where, perhaps, right and wrong are synonyms;
With live bullets, determined, without due regard,
He aimed his gun, with obvious intent, and fired
At students, and apparently they had committed a sin,
The food was bad but they had no right to complain.

That sad event always bothers me when I think
How selfish and fierce human kind can sink,
When he lets money or racism control the rest,
And when man of God forget their religious post
That declares the equality of all man in the eyes of God;
As for the black child, he needed not to be told
Where his allocated position in life stood
He had to keep clear from the law's malicious hand.

The heart that spells the truth is light,
And the truth itself is an eternal light,
No matter how much the truth can hurt,
The truth will set free a sad and burdened heart,
When all looks gloomy and hope is set to flee,
The truth quickly spreads for everyone to see;
He harmed the students he was meant to protect
They refused the badly cooked porridge and meat.

The students took to the heels at gun thunder,
And sanity melted into thin air altogether;
In panic some students landed on barbed wire,

8

While others, their fear turned to anger,
Pelted the dining hall windows with stones,
Smashing, in the process, all the windows to pieces;
They shut down the gen set, the only source of power,
They paid a heavy price for the misdemeanour.

As the gun thundered three times in succession,
One student received a bullet which lodged in his spine,
Another, in his stomach, a bullet was buried,
Yet the other, survived a bullet that grazed his head;
They had crossed the line into the forbidden zone,
Whereas they were of the lower class born,
But the New Testament testifies in the Old book,
Without doubt at all upon which to brook,
But the Brother had a stronger case at hand to maintain,
What is sin, when greed, mammon, power are at stake!
Their demand for better food had a price tag, a mistake.

Regardless of the heinous deed of the previous day,
The Brother knelt before the alter the following day
To receive the body of Christ in Holy Communion
Because he confessed to the priest, his sin was forgiven-
What an unsound but convenient belief for evil doers!
They live between sin and the priests' cubicles,
But almighty God forgives the heart that truly repents.

A DYING NATION

A leader who boasts of his leadership
When many of his people in the country have little hope,
When the country cannot survive unless donations flow,
When the social fabric of the nation is being torn apart
As poverty, hunger, everywhere, dictate moral conduct
And the nation's cultural values diminish, are lost,
Leaving the nation wanting in self discipline and morals,
When a leader encourages lawlessness to set in,
The result will show the true signs of a dying nation.

A country's leader who can hold his head high,
And claim shamelessly to his people, to the whole world,
That he is a true leader, the nation's head,
When many of his people of curable diseases die
When many of his people are destitute,
And others battle with little success to make ends meet
For basic needs for themselves, for their families,
In a country with lean and unsound economies,
In a country that is tottering in brink of total collapse,
While he edges people to point a finger at some else,
And he and the privileged class dine in cheers,
And the cohorts happily feast and wag their tails,
That pales the perception of any commonsense,
The monstrous tabulations are signs of a dying nation.
Therefore every man woman must rise up to his or her station
To cause the government to take its responsibility
And eradicate hunger and poverty.

Many people in the country have been rendered destitute
By people they elected to represent them in government;
Some, shrivelled, squat on pavements and at street corners
And others hang at shop fronts, commuter stations, food outlets,
All over the country- in villages, towns, cities, you name it,
As beggars, while in body and mind they are whole and fit
To fend for themselves, to make a home and raise a family,
But unfortunately they have lost most of their dignity;
The existing system, born of selfishness, avarice and might,

Embraced false wood and ignored outright the poor's plight,
And led the country's economy to a painful grinding halt,
And the government, lying, denies outright that it is at fault.

How can some people be regarded as squatters in their country!
By the country's elected government in an independent country,
Deemed democratic nation state by its leadership, government,
And regarded by foreign governments as a democratic state;
The matter rests on who gives the qualification as a democracy,
Therefore even a dying nation is given the status of democracy!

Beggars have made public open areas permanent homes,
Live without clean water for drinking or cleaning themselves,
Without blankets but their torn clothing face the chilly night,
Face the hard concrete, irritating mosquito bites every night,
And utilise water in public toilets, public parks, nearby streams,
Consequently, many die of hunger and cold and disease,
While their leader dines and sleeps quietly in his mansion
And he remains oblivious of the obvious signs of a dying nation.

Many capable young man, young women, regrettably,
Roam the streets wretched, begging for food or money;
Some, for self sustenance, sadly, take to robbery,
Others flee away to take refuge in foreign countries,
Others flee to countries far beyond for greener pastures,
Many die from political motivated murder, curable diseases,
While the country's leader allocates colossal sums of money
For defence to strength his ruthless coercive machinery,
Not linked to national security nor to poverty alleviation,
That is an obvious sign of a dying nation.

LAND GRAB

Our father used to complain about our new field
That was in an area where we were forcefully settled
And fenced all round with boughs of thorny bushes,
Interwoven to bar both domestic and wild animals
From eating up our crops, our source of lively wood,
In an area where previously only wild animals lived,
And the surrounding thin forest had some lofty trees
And was habitat for herb eaters, many types of birds.

Every morning except Sunday and Wednesday-
The days each of which was held as secret day-
I woke up about three o'clock morning to prepare,
Whenever the moon was up and the sky was bare,
The ploughing equipments to harness the oxen,
Two ploughs for four spans with well bred oxen,
While our sisters prepared the seeds for the field;
I with my elder brother then set off to the field,
Our sisters, carrying packed relief food and seeds,
Balanced on their heads, trailed on our heels;
Often the moon was shining, as we walked with one mind
To till the land, our mother and father followed behind.

Three miles away from our home our field lay,
In a land composed mainly of sand soil and clay,
A field five hundred meters long, ninety meters wide,
In which I, my elder brother, sisters, our parents toiled,
Where previously deciduous and thorn trees grew
And on which couch grass, weeds abundantly grew,
Where after the rains a number of pools would form
And for weeks on end pools of water were a problem
That led to rotting of most of planted seeds
Or to suffocation of our growing crops,
The toughest task was the tilling of the wet clay soils.

In half our field grew, in abundance, couch grass
With its numerous roots running in all directions,
Meandering below the subsoil, in twist and turns;

12

The couch grass made a mesh of roots in the ground,
They rendered working in the field a nightmare indeed.

Oftentimes our field was very dry late in winter,
Still, we tilled most part of our field late in winter,
And the daring feat was the tilling of yawning clay,
I would sweat from start to end of shift for the day.
We ploughed early to avoid mud, stagnant rainwater,
The rest of the field we ploughed early in summer,
And, by hand, we planted seeds throughout the field.
When heavy rains fell, the field became flooded
And for weeks on end remained pools of rainwater,
That threatened, we might die of hunger,
The rainwater took weeks to drain into the ground,
Therefore, from our field we reaped a small yield.

We once lived in a land fit for livestock, crops, I remember
A land talked about so well, so often by my father,
A land where my father was born, my ancestors were buried,
A land that had adequate water supply, fertile soil and
Where livestock flourished on good and plentiful grass,
Where our livestock grazed without danger from predators,
But from where the whole community was forcibly removed
And replaced by white settlers from abroad,
They were allocated a large stretch of land apiece
The blacks were settled in areas with poor soils by force.

Due to land grab by white settlers we were deprived
Of our land, driven away by force, ruthlessly into the wild,
And regrettably, we left our land, left our ancestors graves
Open to desecration, wilfully or not, by cruel white settlers,
And for the loss of our home we received no settlement;
Our new land, with erratic rainfall, was an animal habitat,
Where our live stock died of previously unknown diseases,
And, also, became easy prey for numerous new predators.

ONE-MAN-ONE-VOTE

He spoke to the masses in all regions of the country
That he would fight for independence until victory,
Regardless of the nature of obstacles on the way,
That the struggle would be treacherous all the way,
And he called upon the masses, all his followers,
To stand firm at all odds until intransigent settlers
Accepted what was inevitable, one-man-one-vote,
The election of a true representative government
That transcended colour, race, ethnicity and religion,
And he foretold that some people among them
That elected him to lead the struggle to freedom
Would reject him and branch off along the way,
But that he would not give up, he would persevere,
And along the way would come young generation
And the struggle would continue until freedom was won.

He was flexible and often willing to compromise,
But avarice and power do not need commonsense;
They looked down upon him as a stumbling block,
Bungled him and his colleagues into prison to brook
The consequences for disregard of the rule of law
That was designed to perpetuate the status quo,
He urged people to remain vigilant and patient
The regime was bound to have internal division at last
And would be obliged to release them from prison;
His people too suffered although in an open prison.
The regime had wealth and power but lived in fear
And its followers were sceptical, the end was near.

The oppressor vowed eloquently to stay in power,
He got cheerful applause from every white voter,
Since they had fertile land for all their vast farms,
They had indigenous cheap labour for their factories.
He swore, telling his followers and the whole world,
Natives wouldn't govern the country as long as he lived,
But such wishful thinking fuelled the pace to freedom,
The struggle intensified to unseat the oppressive regime.

The indigenous was deprived of his right to choose,
Except his family, his life, he had nothing to lose;
When hope is lost, when there is nothing to defend,
The future is bleak and life has reached a dead end;
They couldn't tarry anymore, they had to fight
For their right to representation by one-man-one-vote,
Their will power drove them forward against domination,
They had to defend their right to self determination.

They massed streets in towns, cities on peaceful march
In protest against lake of jobs, wages that did not match
Those paid to white employees on equivalent position,
And against all forms of discrimination and oppression;
They carried an olive branch, demanding in unison
To be heard in their plea for freedom and justice for all,
But the regime's army sent them scurrying for survival.

The oppressive regime blindly refused to compromise,
Declared war against opposition that cost property and lives,
That dragged for years as the setter regime, day in day out
Ran constantly its propaganda machine within and without,
Claiming victory against the people's liberation army
That had already established its bases in the country.

The settler regime, driven by its unshakable utopian belief
In essence, nothing more than a buffoon's relief,
That white men, by Almighty God's will, were superior
To black men or somehow blacks happened to be inferior,
Rejected the notion that black men and white men in fact
Should to be regarded as equals before the, law without
A semblance of doubt, just as a baboon is a baboon,
So is the human being, no matter the colour of his skin.

CRIES FOR JUSTICE AND PEACE

Tell me, all you who advocate for war,
Since you talk of peace but opt for war,
When reason instead should to prevail
To serve man against self inflicted peril,
Why you can't be accused for existing turmoil;
Let me hear the civilised people voice,
Without pretentious or coined alliance,
That wily ignores killing of man by man for gain,
And taint freedom and justice for all men
Why they can't be blamed for suffering of man.

You must the truth all of you who claim to know,
Since many people refuse the status quo,
(But where there is smoke there is fire!)
And they still have hope, they won't surrender,
Why, against the people, you support the status quo;
And let me hear from all who are well read,
Since many people are now beggars for food,
The privileged in power enhance their power
Against nonexistent enemies to guard their power,
Why they can't be accused for subverting people's power.

Let honest learned people uphold the law,
Live by example for everyone to follow,
To adhere to norms related to true justice,
The land is crying for freedom, justice and peace
Where all persons are equal before the law
And the people should decide when to wage a war.

I disagree that any war can be regarded as just,
Neither is the killing of a human being ever just,
But I believe that logic and sheer common sense
And sincere dialogue begets justice, lusting peace;
Pre-emptive war, should never be regarded as just,
Neither can any war itself be truthfully ever just,
But want and greed are enemies of justice, peace,
And freedom from want leads to lasting peace.

16

People will fight always against subjugation
By tooth and nail to regain their power,
And they will resist any form of oppression,
Regardless of how powerful the perpetrator,
Until they obtain their freedom against domination.

THE DICTATOR

He who loves peace can very well run the affairs a nation,
He who becomes a leader by power usurpation
Becomes a mindless dictator that leads his country to ruin,
Awards even crooked people to consolidate his power,
Makes dubious alliances with some foreign power
To the detriment of his country, wishes of his people,
He is prone to suppress any dissent with an iron rule,
Behind the scenes he dines with enemies of his people
And sacrifices his country's affairs for personal gain,
He looks upon himself as the only person fit to reign.

How does a people's elected leader become a monster!
But I know for certain that a thief in his trade is a master,
A self imposed leader, by nature of his status, is a dictator,
While an imperialist will always yearn for his lost empire;
And politics, as I see it, will always corrupt the corruptible
And corrupted politics can cause a country, to crumble.
The dictator will always defend his corrupted misrule
By descending upon dissent by the people with guile,
Well orchestrated to induce fear, either by coercion,
Or through his well oiled propaganda machine
That often becomes a killer like a deadly disease,
The nation painfully crumbles from its leader's ruse.

Often a self imposed leader springs up as a surprise,
Ascends the political ladder with lightning speed and ease,
The sudden rise to power is soon welcome by some empire,
And leaders of the same feather congratulate the new comer.

Just as I liken a wicked man's gift to a thief's gift
So is the gift that comes with strings attached to it;
It is not a secret that also crocodiles do lay eggs
But with them comes attached the enemy's artifice
To lay enemy's foundation for fettered economic regime,
Intended to hold forever the governing regime at ransom,
While the enemy erodes the core of the nation's strength
By relentlessly plundering the country's wealth,

But the imposed leader delights in money and power,
He remains blind as long as his position is secure.

Once in power the leader soon becomes a millionaire,
He creates strong coercive instruments, he employs to snare
The people whom he fears are likely to contend for power
And to silence dissenting voices he might encounter,
While the people lose representation as per democratic rule
And their standard of living diminishes, becomes unbearable,
With the passage of time the empire's wile is laid bare,
The people ferociously demand exit of the imposed leader.

A dictator always lives under self generated fear,
Since the oppressive nature of his rule breeds fear
Of enemies who are both real and nonexistent,
And the majority of citizens his rule do dissent,
And trust is a word he would not dare to hear,
And many people in his country live in perpetual fear
Of the state, the unjust and oppressive rule of law,
Where the oppressive regime is protected by law,
Where law protects interests of privileged people,
Where prejudice per political affiliation, race, tribe prevail
And where punishment for mere decent is very severe
To cow into submission the people through fear;
He turns government into his personal mouth piece
To the detriment of national stability and justice,
And sets, covertly, state power against the people
And strengthens, at all costs, his unwanted misrule
But in consequent he destroys the fabric of the nation
And he drastically undermines national aspiration.

A dictator's subjects must obey, without question, his rule
And adhere to the rules he has set for them and be loyal,
Lest they be found wanting and be imprisoned for dissent,
A dictator, oftentimes, attains leadership as a patriot
And with colourful speech he promises heaven on earth-
Democracy, liberty, justice, peace and so forth,
But soon his promises begin to melt into thin air,
His personal ambitions steadily but surely begin to bear,

While the army, the police are meticulously politicised
And independence, freedom, justice become marginalised;
To ensure his power, the dictator enlists some foreign force
From leaders willing to enhance their sphere of influence
And consequently lands the country on a political dilemma
As the country's economy slowly sinks into a quagmire,
And the country is destabilised, becomes ungovernable;
And the dictator's greed for power becomes insatiable,
But a dictator's coercive system is always alert
And effectively armed and ready to strike at any cost,
With uttermost force and horrid spite,
Against anyone, anywhere, at any time,
If anyone dares challenge his totalitarian rule,
And the dictator's threat is always real,
And he can strike a fatal blow at his will.

A good nation's leader governs through the peoples will,
In accordance with people's power surrenders his rule,
And he is rightly honoured by his people ever after,
But a dictator subdues the nation and governs by force,
And his unwanted misrule in consequence ends in misery.

CAPITALISM

I am compelled to embrace capitalism
Even though I am just a common man,
I learned to cherish the power of money
Though I had no capital to make money,
But I have had a sad feeling all along,
And I would like the alarm to be rung
That erosion of human co-existence,
Diminishing demand for moral values,
Disregard of the essence of human dignity,
One of the important pillars of all humanity
Misconception of the purpose of human life
That binds us with God, with the spiritual life,
And the woes due to greed and power
That make the less privileged poorer
Should be eradicated, at all costs, at once,
To serve man from self inflicted injustice.
And as capital directs, dictates all the rules
And money and greed and power resonate,
The rich exploit the poor for maximum profit,
Since labour of so many creates riches for so few,
And fair play by people in power is never due,
Labourers often live on morsels after sweat,
While the rich gather to dine and celebrate.

I wish I could define free market enterprise
In relation to cost of goods workers produce,
The actual value of the total services available,
Where distribution of goods, services is equitable;
I hear, capitalism entails free market enterprise,
But through exploitation of labour capitalism thrives
Where most people have no access to capital
And are held at bay by the system, to fulfil
The roll of keeping labour everywhere in excess
So as monopolise the market for maximum profits.

When only a few people hold massive capital,
Where the market is totally free, the law of the jungle!

The average man labours and fails to make ends meet,
Capitalists control covertly operations of government,
But I cannot argue at all with the professionals,
Whereas I can argue successfully with my equals
That there is a definite peculiar flaw in the system
That distorts, obviously, democracy as a system.

I do not believe any person finds the idea disputable
That all human beings are by nature sociable,
And the Bible gives clear and concise admonition
By the Almighty God who is in heaven
That man must love his neighbour always
And do to his neighbour at all times
What he would want his neighbour do to him always.

GREEDY AND POWERFUL

The wicked must quickly give away their wicked way,
Since there will be no time for repentance on that day,
Desires and glories of this world will come to naught
And there will be no space for greed, power and might,
But everyone's past thoughts, deeds will be the matter,
When the Almighty God will all his sheep timely gather
And the wicked He will cast away into the burning fire.

A kind heart will always carry a serene face,
Even when the going is hard under the surface,
While a callous heart is overburdened with hate,
Of its wickedness creates enemies at every street;
But every person has his own free will to choose
And if you believe in God you have nothing to lose,
And a person's will is the almighty's deliberate gift
To all man big and small, rich and poor, and the gift
Enables man to choose between good and evil,
But if man chooses evil, chooses it at his own peril.

I wish I were that man with a big and open heart,
That man of abundant goodwill and excellent spirit,
The man who acquires his money and his material wealth
By exploiting, fairly, the numerous materials with
Or through his own diligence and acquired wisdom
(The knowledge that can create a beautiful home),
But I dread that crooked man with a callous heart,
The avaricious man who preys on other people's sweat,
The man who amasses money, wealth by crooked means
And uses his wealth to tread upon other people's rights,
That man who exploits his neighbour shamelessly
And who adores his wealth and his power even blindly.

When power is begotten of greed in a system,
Exploitation of man by man will remain the norm,
When the rich take pride on greed, power and might
The poor, on small income, fail to make ends meet,
And the greatest enemy of ordinary man becomes fear,

A product of oppression and insecurity in the sphere
Of influence by the greedy and powerful who run the state,
Until fear is overtaken at last by dissent, anger and spite.

ILLUSTROUS SON

Let the sun disappear with its bright light,
And the moon and the stars pale at night;
Doom has struck the cornerstone of our home,
They must at least write explicitly an epitome
In order to inform all the generations to come,
His love for his country, the nation, the children;
He fought for freedom, equity and peace for the nation.

The colourful leopard which from the enemy disappeared,
Only to announce from where he was less expected,
The man who at his young age surprised the elders,
When he was lost in the wild for several days,
Only to be found high on a tall tree, alive, seated,
That was, to everybody present, a mystery indeed!
He was a man, not afraid for his life in a moment of need
And he faced all his adversaries with courage indeed.

The river of hope has dried, it is no more!
We inherit a harrowing, an unbearable sore,
Let us all kneel and pray to heaven above,
Since the man, the leader, the symbol of love,
The man with an unblemished desire to serve,
The fountain of hope with marked decency,
The beacon of equity, freedom, untainted justice,
The man whose principles clearly stood for peace,
The man who was accessible but not impervious
To the opinions of others, no matter their status,
The man who was, for everyone's delight, a shining star
When everything looked insurmountable, dire,
The man whose power embodied people's respect,
Since it was founded upon the people's support,
The man who weighed his tongue at all times
Even when his adversaries called him names,
The man who spoke to the point about what was due,
In accordance with his belief and the people's view
And who accepted blame for wrong decisions he made;
His soul has departed, in short, the man is dead.

It is a sad day, a day that shall never be forgotten;
The nation moans the passing of its illustrious son,
The tears will flow until their source is exhausted
But the hearts, for the great loss, shall for ever bleed,
Millions of people, unable to go to the burial site,
Line along streets in cities to lay their last respect,
As the funeral procession passes towing the hearse
And even his enemies have come to give reverence,
While they envied, chided him when he was alive;
Today they will not hide and their lies shall not live,
Else the nation will be shuttered, broken to pieces,
And with their lies they can't bind together the pieces.

From villages, towns, cities, every corner of the country
People, in thousands, flood the country's capital city,
Transported by buses, trains, private cars, other means,
Heading to the nation's burial place for national heroes;
The people pour still in great numbers unseen before,
His enemies gaze agape in awe, in disbelieving wonder,
At the spectacle that gives witness to the whole world-
The clear testimony, the man was a great man indeed.

He was a great leader with a great heart and a patron,
Let them that knew him well testify to all the children,
To the nation, to the whole world about the man himself,
How he loved his people and about his political life,
They must leave no stone unturned in their testimony;
He struggled, suffered for the independence of the country
But his enemies cannot utter his name even in death
Though it is needless for them to tarry from the truth,
Since no matter how much ugly, bitter the truth can be,
The truth heals the wound, the soul, sets the heart free.
He was called father of the nation once, spirits know that,
Let the Lord above, welcome his beloved spirit.
The leader is dead, his work, his name shall never be forgotten
And his good work must chart an excellent future for the nation.

The hero has passed away but his spirit is not gone,
It is with us, in our hearts, to encourage us to carry on

With the most important work of building up the nation,
While doing so we should always take into account,
We remain humble, honest, diligent and tolerant.

A NIGHTMMARE

He held both my hands pressed on my back
With both his hands gripping firmly my hands,
So firm was the grip that I could not break
Free from my assailant, my effort was hopeless,
I screamed and screamed and screamed,
Suddenly I heard bang, bang, bang, I screamed;
The bang was not a dream; I lay and listened hard.
When I opened my eyes the room was dark,
The terrifying nock at the door shook the house
And dreadful insults rained without a break,
Followed by an order, I should open the door at once;
With sweat dripping I stared at nothing,
And shaken, shivering from the voice threatening,
I lit, with a match stick, a paraffin lamp in silence.

Then, I was aware, that was not a nightmare,
I dressed up quickly and with my feet bare,
My mind racing, I staggered to the door
To face the dreadful intruder,
I was afraid but I had to open the door,
And I could not delay for a minute longer;
Armed with a rifle the intruder at the door backed
When I stepped out of the door, I tumbled.

I suspected, he was not alone, there were others,
Holding the lamp I stood face to face
With an armed stubby man with piercing eyes,
Suddenly I saw a bright light in my right eye
As his open hand landed a stunning blow
That sent me flying to the ground, but I
Quickly picked myself up before a boot could follow,
Almost confused, I scanned the darkness beyond,
In a blink of an eye, I found myself surrounded
By several men, armed with automatic rifles
Menacingly equipped with bayonets,
Then, I noticed, they were freedom fighters.

THE BUFFALO

I was not new on the job but on the route
That ploughed its way across the game territory
For hundreds of kilometres straight,
Through the largest game reserve in the country
Where the herb eaters and predators
Lived with less human interference;
I nearly died because of ignorance.

I have had many people say before,
That ignorance always has no defence,
I wish I had the capacity this notion to deplore,
Even the guilty, before proven guilty, claim innocence;
I disembarked from the locomotive at one o'clock at night,
Sent by the driver to phone the operator about the red light,
At the telephone booth I became afraid
When I saw animals move in the shadows of night.

On the other side the operator was alarmed,
He warned me against getting off at the location,
And he directed that we ignore the red light
And wait for the departure light at the station,
I felt shiver creeping through my skin,
Light, I walked back, somehow I didn't run,
I had, unaware, ventured into the wild beasts' den!

What I had seen, at night, at the telephone both,
Gave me a shock of my life in the morning,
And questions raced in my mind, I felt a surge of wrath;
He had sent me to phone, aware of what could be lacking?
He knew the area well, yet he sent me to a head of buffalo!
There was nothing for him to benefit by my death;
I gazed agape, a head of buffalo grazed near the water hole.

If I had been killed, he had all the defence!
I should have known, we were in the game reserve,
He could not be blamed for my ignorance,
If the buffalo had charged I was unlikely to survive,

And who would stand on my behalf against him,
Since, the privileged often are immune to blame,
But the system itself hangs on an edge of doom.

INDEPENDENCE

They were under the auspices of a foreign power,
They fought hard for the country's independence
And celebrated their freedom, cattle were put to slaughter,
Jubilee parties in the country sent echoes of happiness,
But the spirits of people who lost in the election were low,
Defeat in any contest sometimes is hard to swallow
And dissent against the winner remains a constant sore.

The country's independence came after a bitter
Struggle, but the colonial chain remained intact,
Attached to all the essential elements of real power;
The independence they won was shaky, inconsistent,
But the leader was hailed by the imperial ruler
And the so called civilised world hailed him louder;
He shunned those who gave him help forever.

It is painful to be known to be free yet not free,
Even if you cry for help, the help will not come,
Since you have made your bed you cannot flee;
You have your leader, your independence, your freedom.
In subterfuge they helped you to lead there,
But latter threw spanners in your works there
So that when you are done they rebuild everything there.

They knew that greed and power built the empire,
That people's freedom and the expansion of justice
Eroded and shook the foundations of the empire;
But the country had regained partial independence,
Since the country's economic structure
Was designed to conform to imperial whim and desire
To protect its wealth, it's kin, their wealth and welfare.

The independence was won through sweat and blood,
The struggle still continues today, will continue tomorrow,
To uproot the imperial gnawing, grinding root of greed,
The cause for inequality among people before the law
People want their independence they fought for and won,
Their complaint has been loud and clear, they are wan
About dwelling in the past when the future is bleak, let it be known.

31

SUCH WICKEDNESS

They were all young women, not combat soldiers,
Under training for civic duty for the nation;
Having fled their country in fear for their lives,
They thought, they had a chance to obtain education,
But the vicious enemy, in his wicked way, followed them
In the bushes of a foreign country, far from their home,
When they hoped, at last, they would obtain freedom.

Unexpectedly, a deafening blast rent the air,
Followed by another and another and another;
The enemy's fighter jets roared, spat death and fear,
People, trees and the ground were torn asunder,
The earth vibrated from the deafening gun fire;
The devil had landed, then was followed by evil,
They killed young women, defenceless young people.

They landed by choppers and hunted them down,
With explosives, they buried some in their hide out,
Others who tried to escape they sprayed them down
With bullets, others they netted, paraded for heinous amusement,
The scars on their corpses gave witness to them
Who saw the corpses, even heaven could shy away for shame!
They committed the crime on the stool of God's kingdom.

GREED

Let me extend my hand with ease,
Without any strings attached or hidden motive,
To assist other people who need assistance,
For every person needs another to well survive,
As a matter of fact, it's neither here nor there,
The wealthy use capital to exploit workers anywhere
And their riches expand from the workers' labour.

Greed stops at nothing to meet its desire for material wealth,
It tramples on everything, everybody on its way to riches
And it creates a chain of ruins along its path,
Noticeable by sight of beggars, pickpockets, homelessness,
The less privileged have very little or nothing to ferry home,
But the bible testifies, it's hard for rich men to enter God's kingdom,
The righteous obtain material wealth by diligence and wisdom.

Let scholars, intellectuals tell us what they mean by fair play,
Regarding the economic world and the rights of man,
Since all comes to naught when greed charts its way;
Instead they join the band wagon in exploitation of men,
And women and children everywhere suffer the most,
And family ties and discipline and morals are lost,
And love among people disappears, is supplanted by lust.

Greed is greed, no matter your perception,
The effects of greed are as clear as a cloudless sky:
Ambiguously, wars are waged but truly for gain,
Civil disobedience becomes the order of the day,
The hardened heart with its insatiable desire for wealth sinks low,
While it seeks for more and more and more,
The hardened heart adores it wealth forevermore.

Greed! You are monster that erodes the fabric of humanity,
How easy it is for you to receive than to give!
What belongs to you is bitter, to another is tasty,
You need purgation, excision, as much as I believe.

POWER

I am hapless and my spirit is low,
Everything around me is remote and forsaken,
The whole world is lifeless, an empty burrow;
What is there to live for! All my hope is gone,
Wherever I turn I see darkness and gloom,
Everything I touch turns to dust;
My situation, in all aspects, is dire and grim,
Let the power of the spirit strengthen my heart,
I want, against all odds, to achieve my dream;
I am stripped of everything, of all power,
Even the right to exercise my will power,
But Almighty above will restore my power.

When I feel lost, when hope is on the fringe,
I seek God's endless power, hope is sustained,
My heart is invigorated against the horrid deluge
Of corrupt earthly power, begot, enhanced by greed.
The privileged class hold the means of power,
The heartless power that knows no honour,
Often power does not listen to reason altogether.

I need power to achieve my intended goals,
I needed power yesterday, I need power today;
My will to serve, to shoulder on still prevails,
But obstacles always stand on my way;
Let the power, driven by the will of God,
I don't need mammon or the power born of greed,
Drive me to fulfil the purpose of my life in this world.

SCORNFUL EYES

On honey moon we tour the Water Falls,
We book at one of the most elegant hotels
At the tourist resort we both longed to see;
We go late to bed, get up in the morning with glee,
With unprecedented high expectation
For a great day, full of perfect exhilaration,
But I am in for a surprise as we sit at breakfast,
When I see a visitor I least expect-
Now I have a feeling, we are being watched
By the regime's agents, dreaded, black eyed,
Known for arresting blacks on flimsy suspicions
And send them to lounge in hellish prisons,
He introduces himself as a foreigner,
But I recognise him as a police inspector.
With a smile, he unveils his passport,
I am taken aback because I know who he is,
The affected smile he gives is conspicuous,
And I have misgivings, something bad is afoot,
I decide not to air my suspicions to my wife,
Our honey moon could be marred by fear for my life.

He extends his hand, with a dubious smile,
In greeting, shakes hands with me and my wife
But somehow, in my mind, I gleam a hidden lie,
Also my heart tells me, my wife is not at ease,
At a glance I see her doubtful furtive eye-
(By design, whites can't shake hands with blacks),
But likewise we acknowledge his greetings.

The blue sky is clear but a lonely milky cloud,
Hanging low to the north east above the trees,
There is a promise of a beautiful sunny day ahead.
Enticing scenery of the hotel's large open ground
With well cut green lawn and beautiful flowers,
And a magnificent swimming pool, fifty paces away
And facing the hotel's back entrance way,
Give a splendid view of the whole premises;

At the swimming pool we meet scornful eyes,
All the visitors at the swimming pool are whites,
We look at each other in instant bewilderment
And we retreat to avoid needless embarrassment.

I AM PROHIBITED

I take leave of the village into the city,
Enough money I have to give myself a treat
In one pub I often admire at a distance,
A pub with a beautiful artistic entrance;
As I enter I am arrested and fascinated
By its spacious area that is superbly furnished,
And by its exhilarating, cool, rich, fresh air;
A soft green carpet covers the floor area,
And brown sofas, coffee tables, all splendid,
As if straight from the carpenter's hand,
Are arranged nicely to leave free space
For free movement for servants and customers;
High cushioned mahogany stools line at the counter,
Beyond the counter lies the inviting liquor,
Above the counter the spot lights are hung
And along the wall shines brilliant up-lighting,
While the ceiling gives pleasant down-light;
The lighting gives inviting environment.

Sadly, the pub is reserved for white customers
By order, and the present clientele also testifies
Non whites are not allowed;
Therefore, in the premises, I am prohibited,
Because of the colour of my skin,
I cannot dine where white men dine,
I cannot sit where white men sit,
Nor can I use a cup, beer glasses, you name it;
All the waiters, waitresses, in the pub, are non whites,
They serve food, drinks, wash kitchen utensils.

THE RESTAURANT

In the restaurant they let me buy coke and pie,
When I sat to drink my coke and eat the pie,
A waitress approached, whispered in my ear-
"Only white customers are allowed in here"
Then, a young man burst with a queer laughter,
As he pointed to a notice beyond the counter;
All eyes were on me as I stood there baffled,
Bereft of any ideas on how to respond;
They gaped at me as if I was some apparition,
Descended among them from a place unknown;
I took a step back and turned to walk away,
And collided with an old lady in my dismay,
The ground felt shaky, uneven under my feet,
As I walk away from the scene into the street.

I hated myself for having taken the chance,
When I clearly had noticed from a distance
That the clientele was all white;
I earned my humiliation, my embarrassment!
I was lost why the justification for the anomaly
That there must be places reserved for whites only;
I still had my food, the cause of my embarrassment,
Since the law prohibited eating in the street.

WE HAD BROKEN THE ICE

The sun had just passed mid-day in spring
When we arrived, having left home in the morning,
The sun was peeping through the grey clouds
That were floating in the sky ever southwards;
In the hotel grounds a few tall deciduous trees
Were still blooming with colourful flowers,
Enhancing the beautiful landscape of the hotel,
Built on slightly higher ground facing an open space
Five hundred paces to the game reserve's water hole;
The trees that dotted the hotel's open area
And the green lawn and flower beds in the premises,
They released nice aroma that enriched the air.

A sizable number of visitors occupied the paved area
That was large enough to accommodate a lot of people
And located at the front entrance of the hotel,
Some visitors sat at round tables
Drinking alcohol or some soft drinks,
While a few stood here and there chatting
All were in happy spirits, amicably admiring
The view and animals at the water hole drinking,
The hotel had only black waitresses and waiters,
My girl-friend and I were the only black visitors,
When I noticed, among the visitors, none was black.

To ascertain we were allowed I asked a waiter,
She whispered to me, non whites were barred;
Then, I sought confirmation from the manager,
My polite inquiry, at least, it seemed,
As much as I could read from the manager's face,
To have caught the manager completely off guard,
He hesitated, looking directly into my eyes,
Then, he said, we were very much welcome,
And, with a smile, added, we should feel at home
And that the hotel was at our good service;
Then, I told my girl-friend, we had broken the ice.

THE TURNING POINT

The settler regime had on power clung
And its economic power remained strong
Regardless of economic sanctions by the world body,
That, wily imposed, affected everybody;
The poor, the indigenous bore the greatest brunt
(The ants suffer the most when elephants fight);
But the indigenous couldn't be cowed by sanctions,
They stood firm against the regime's machinations,
They struggled fearlessly for one-man-one-vote;
The war had evidently taken too many lives,
The imperial power called for urgent talks,
They signalled the struggle's turning point.

They were on a campaign to destroy, kill and maim
The freedom fighters who had gained momentum
In the battle for independence;
The regime vowed to uproot them at their bases,
Including at their bases in neighbouring countries,
But that was easier said than done,
As the regime's casualties of that day have shown;
The attacking planes, in broad day light,
In a massive show of force, hit the camp sight,
It signalled the settler regime's wrath,
With heavy bombardment, gun-fire that rocked the earth,
Rent the air, the sound echoed on the gorges
And filled the whole air space,
Sent splinters of rock flying into the air,
Tore tree stems, branches, threw them everywhere,
But the settler regime's target was void
Because the regime was outwitted,
The freedom fighters' return fire was intense, accurate,
The settler regime was hit right, centre and left;
The regime's bombers disappeared in flames
And their Ring Leader was buried in flames,
His plane, shot down, exploded in the gorges.

The regime's fighter helicopters appeared

From all sides of the mountainous ground,
Hoping to find the freedom fighters in disarray,
But that was not to be that day;
The freedom fighters were well armed, in position
And expecting the enemy from any direction,
They were alert on mountains above, in gorges below,
Choppers met hell fire from mountains above and below,
And they were subsequently blown
And their human content sent to oblivion,
Choppers couldn't land nor escape the onslaught,
They were, from all directions, by gun fire, hit
And exploded, sending smoke, flame into the air,
The whole area smelt of gun powder and sizzling fire.

DISSIDENT'S CHILD

Defenceless and petrified she moaned,
As scourges and fists and boots rained
Continuously, viciously on the fragile woman,
Accused of being pregnant of a dissident;
They were content in tormenting a pregnant woman,
And they seemed to enjoy their wicked act,
In the process they uttered torrent of obscene language.

They were huddled together under siege,
After having been forced out of the bus
By a brutal, wrathful, heavily armed force;
Man groaned, women and children screamed
As they were being beaten, brutalised,
And some, terrified, silently gave prayer,
As they glared at the unfolding dreadful nightmare,
Many of them with clothes already drenched in blood
That trickled from multiple wounds to soak the earth
And with broken ribs and broken teeth;
Some, begged for mercy, on their knees,
Their tormentors gave deaf ears to their pleas.

When the pregnant woman's stomach was split,
On grassy dirty ground, her blood, internals spilled,
Followed by the wailing of women, holding their heads,
Their tears having dried up in utter hopelessness.

She lay still on her blood, she was dead,
Beside her lay dead foetus of her eight months pregnancy,
And the soldiers, seemingly delighted,
They had killed the unborn dissident's child,
And without the least feeling of remorse,
Toward the dead innocent woman and the wounded,
Threw insults at people they had brutalised,
And shouting, rowdy, oblivious to their felonious deed,
They boarded their trucks and departed;
Their heinous sin they shall carry to judgement day.

4
MY INTRODUCTION

The setting sun, on the horizon, was an orange ball
As the freedom fighters bade us farewell
When we climbed over the fence at the border;
We entered the neighbouring country to the south;
At a fast pace we walked well into the night
On a small path, near the border, toward south
To avoid being lost in the animal habitat;
We took the path none of us had used before,
We walked in fear of being apprehended by the foe.

Determined I was, we should not stop on the way
Until we reached the chief's village,
We agreed to stay together all the may
If on the way we chose to sleep,
In any village, in one room we should sleep.

We walked as fast as our legs could carry us,
We had walked the whole day in hot weather,
Then, due to the slightly cold breeze the air had cooled
But we were thirsty we all needed water,
By a stroke of luck, we heard dogs barking,
A few hundred paces from where we were walking,
And in the blue starry sky, the moon was shinning.

The village was shrouded in darkness,
A candle light peeped through door slits
Of one of several huts in the yard
As if the locals had long gone to bed,
Then, a dog barked angrily, another followed,
From somewhere in the yard a man's voice called,
Politely I called back in answer,
He welcomed us and gave us water
But I was shocked to learn from our guest,
The enemy had been seen in the vicinity of late,
Inwardly I cursed, suggested we at once proceed;
I thanked him for hospitality, and off we hurried.

I could guess from their tottering feet,
Their breathing that was heavy and short
And constant turning of their heads to scan the rear
That they were internally embraced in fear;
I was not myself in any situation better,
I had a persistent gnawing reminder,
If the enemy sprung up, the pathetic journey could be over.

At mid-night we arrived at the chief's village,
We were ushered into an empty room,
Then, one female in our group was whisked away,
I and other women had an hour in the gloom,
Latter they took all the women away,
I told our guest, the freedom fighters had shown us the way
Relieved, I was led to the refugee camp the following day

I FROZE

For two days in succession I had had one meal
And close to two hundred miles I had walked
Without rest nor sleep at all,
But my desire to join the armed struggle still held
In strength, in optimism and in spirit,
Nothing could stop me, my mind was set,
When reason fails, by force justice shall be met.

When I arrived at the police station
By lorry, with an exhausted group of fifteen,
At twenty hundred hours,
A large number of my country men,
Weary, gloomy and seemingly lost,
As if their world was a thing of the past,
They were on the line to become refugees at last.

When I registered as refugee unease I felt
Because they retained my identity document,
But somehow I felt a surge of hope,
My prayer had been answered at least,
The time had come to take the bull by the horns!
After registration we put up then
For the night, within the police station

In the morning I woke up, froze and stared
At a person I knew very well as regime's agent,
One of the regime's most feared;
I pretended I didn't know him until the right moment.

MY TRANSFORMATION

The truck was meandering through the forest
As the sun was disappearing to the west,
When I saw countless faces rising from the bushes;
I suspected they were freedom fighters
Though their attire left me uncertain,
And at some paces away their faces were sullen;
My hair stood and a chill ran down my spine
And I felt a mixture of fear and apprehension.
Except for our truck's sound, the world was quiet,
As our truck stopped at a few thatched houses;
As if from nowhere, three armed men appeared,
And in a small thatched house for the night we huddled.

We were forced to declare all our possession,
Some had little money, tooth pastes tooth brushes,
But I had nothing except my clothes I had on;
We were stripped, searched handbags, clothes, purses,
And I observed the scene with rising apprehension;
The fighters spoke unseemly, their language was obscene,
But that marked the beginning of my transformation.

I was at the transit camp for the party's armed wing,
One of many created to fight the oppressive regime;
I was content, I had arrived to assume
My training as a soldier, the following morning,
And the whole night we were huddled in the tiny room,
Through the small window, the night was dark and silent
Except for barking frogs somewhere in the distant forest,
There were thousands of comrades manning the site;
For freedom and justice, they were prepared to fight.

TRIBALISM

My country and its people will always lie
Upon the strongest bond that holds me to my tribe,
Due to traits, traditions and culture that underlie,
And I dance oftentimes to the whims of my tribe;
Lake of conscience, underlying prejudice, do prevail
But I shouldn't discriminate against other people,
All people, in the eyes of God, are equal.

I love my people, my tribe, my race,
I like who I am and the colour of my skin,
Hatred I abhor, no matter what may be the case,
And I know, he who is greedy and covets lives in sin;
My parents gave me love, love dwells in me,
Even in burdensome times my heart is free,
And that is what I would like to be.

I cannot hate nor dislike another person,
But I may like or dislike actions of another person,
Regardless of the extent of your power,
I alone, I am and will always, for what I do,
Be answerable to myself and to others,
But let those who do evil or induce evil power to others
Know they will be judged when God his sheep gathers.

True love frees the heart that is burdened
And cheers the successes of others,
But he who covets is greedy and wicked,
He lays waste anything in his way to enhance his powers,
He pities against each other, peoples- tribes, races or states,
And tribalism is his basest weapon,
He uses it to rob them all of their wealth within.

BURNING HOMES

Painful wailing of women more than a mile away,
Followed by similar cries, erupting closer and closer,
From north, south, east and west, everywhere,
Becoming ever louder and louder and louder,
Accompanied by frenzy, chilly screaming of children,
While locals should have been in bed early at dawn,
They were obvious signals that hell had broken lose.

The sky everywhere was orange-red with flames,
The wailing, screaming of people, mingled with gun fire,
In all directions towards the burning homes,
The stench of burning flesh and the smell of hot fire,
From the blistering inferno, filled the air space;
The people who survived the carnage took to their heels,
They ran from the horrid attack, into the cover of bushes.

The small children that saw the next light,
They were those, their mothers quickly grabbed, gagged
And flew with them silently away into the night,
And those lucky children were very few indeed;
As for the elderly, non survived the army's onslaught,
Unleashed by the ruling elite, the people in power,
They wanted desperately to consolidate their power.

The bid for power threw the country into turmoil,
Divided the indigenous people into tribal factions,
And the enemy threw flames into a situation volatile
That flared in cities, towns and villages,
Causing mayhem and death of innocent people
As the army was deployed against dissidents;
The deposed regime mocked the independence,
It had ushered in civil war and homelessness.

THE RIVER

My life was under threat, I decided on a better option,
I fled the country to evade the regime's secret agents;
The sun had long departed beyond the horizon,
Leaving behind a clear blue sky, decorated with stars
That looked down to mother earth from the far heaven,
And the bright full moon that chased away the darkness;
Shockingly the river was almost fifty paces wide,
The water seemed still, I looked at it with apprehension,
Wondering how I was going to cross to the other side.

About the river I had heard, I did not know its depth,
Also, I was afraid there could be crocodiles inside,
Then, dogs barked beyond the river to the south;
I improvised a long stick to feel the river bed
On my unpredictable way across to the opposite side,
Since I had decided, I could not be a victim of fear,
If my adventure was a failure, then my fate was clear.

When I was close to the edge of the river,
The sand disappeared from under my feet,
As I drifted unconsciously in the water,
Due to under current, to further down the river;
By chance my foot was caught by a tree root,
Then, I let the probing long stick off my hand,
I leaned, in the deepening water, to cling to the root
And I followed the root up to the tree and land.

HE WAS INNOCENT

Early in the morning, at sun-rise,
The army had spread its wings on every village,
But some men, in the village, escaped the noose,
They eluded certain dearth by the thinnest edge;
My uncle did not survive the wicked net,
His wife and children glared in fear and bewilderment
The soldiers tugged him into their truck to his fate.

They were a bunch of heartless brutes,
Their mothers would shy away forever to hear,
They gave birth to such mindless nuts;
Even this selfish, miserable world could leer
At the sycophants, beget of greed, and
Set on their inhuman mission, and
They left a trail of death and destruction.

They off-loaded their truck near the villages,
They forced their victims to dig a large grave,
Then, they shot dead eleven of their victims,
The remaining victim tugged the dead into the grave,
He filled the grave with soil and pile of stones,
After he had buried their sordid deed,
As he stood, sweat dripping from his face,
They shot him on the head, left him for carrion beasts;
He was an innocent man, not a dissident,
And non among them all was a dissident.

AN ENEMY WAS WITHIN

I was standing within a multitude of refugees
That filled a two acre refugee compound,
A home to over six hundred hungry refugees,
In which two large blocks, barely adequate, stood,
And which was surrounded by a fence two metres tall,
Brooding over so many young men, denied a chance
To build a better future for better existence,
They were led to a state so pathetic and miserable;
The regime because of its bigotry lacked commonsense.

A young man, shabby, frightened, seemingly hapless
Shared with me the source of his fright;
He claimed, one of the regime's secret police
Was in the camp as head of the security department,
His tale tallied with the arrest of a man I knew well
And who, sadly, subsequently died in a police cell,
But the camp's leadership didn't receive the message well.

The young man had rubbed feathers with powerful people
By his tale that named the security head as enemy agent,
The young man, his friends, including some people
Who came from his home area, became the target;
They were quickly picked up for questioning,
Transferred to other camps, with tags- unfit combatant,
Accused for rumour mongering;
I became aware then, an enemy was within establishment.

THEY TOLD THEIR ORDEAL

Pity the child who in foreign hands grow,
Their mothers they will never know,
That deep-rooted, motherly everlasting love,
The love which only the natural mother can give,
The new life's permanent umbilical cord,
That ties the natural mother to her child
Is no more, has been shattered.

Pity every child that grows without a father,
Let alone as a refugee in a foreign country,
Since in his heart he misses his father,
The friendship which only a father can proffer,
The hug which makes him loved and protected
And the assurance that makes a home ever homely
Even when the situation all round is bad.

Throughout the country, from ruined homes,
Many children, alone, wretched and forlorn,
Fled through dangerous wild to nearby countries,
Some of the children wandered and got lost in the wild,
Others became victims to wild beasts,
Yet others were swallowed by flooded rivers,
They told their ordeal who reached the refugee camps.

I shudder to think how many children died of disease,
And hunger and thirst and dehydration,
They were bound to lose direction in the wilderness,
Their number is certainly still unknown;
Poverty denied many of the children a normal home,
They were discarded by the corrupt system,
And they were forced to flee from political mayhem;
How hard it is for human kind to attain God's kingdom!

THEY SHUNNED REALITY'S FACE

The settler regime, in anticipation of a people's riot,
Deployed throughout the country and at every street,
Police, army and secret service armed to the teeth,
Determined to crash dissent that dared cross its path;
Instead an exodus of men, women, boys and girls,
Fleeing, single or in small groups, to other countries,
Regardless of intimidation, brutality, including murder borne,
Sneaked with determination past the regime's cordon;
They were all driven by a common compelling desire,
To return home with power to depose the regime by fire
In order to achieve independence, freedom, and justice,

The settler regime failed to weigh existing tension,
Until a surging, relentless and vicious war began,
Because stubbornly they shunned reality's face
And chose confrontation instead of equity and justice,
Through equitable representation which was then inevitable,
The whole country became a battle ground, ungovernable.
While it's easy to start a war, to win it is a bitter lesson.
As the war ragged, boys, girls, farmers, men and women,
Ruthlessly and mercilessly perished on both sides,
Until the settler regime succumbed, declared a truce
And agreed on the road to the country's independence
By the will of the people, based on the popular vote,
People celebrated although the atmosphere was tight.

NOT FOR THE NATION

I had understood clearly what he had said,
That, no doubt, made me very sad indeed,
And I became aware of his intention behind
His flowery speech, counter to what he did.

His rhetoric crossed the deluge with ease!
He said what they wanted to hear, to appease,
And they all clapped hands in great applause,
Because they were blind, they had a lot to lose.

Everything he did, he did it for himself alone,
Not for the nation, but covetous greed spurred him on,
And his accomplices on the loot cheered him on
Finally they had nothing left to loot again.

Why cry! He made his bed, let him lie on his bed,
Let his grand ideas that led to the horrid deed
Unloose him from his fettered end
And his cronies in the loot pay for their wicked deed.

A SOLDIER'S UNIFORM

In the morning, at my door, I heard a knock
The knock was loud and persistent bangs;
My heart pounding, I staggered to look
Through the peephole, and holding my lungs
I scanned the outside and saw my mother,
Quickly I dressed up convinced something sinister
Was afoot from the prevailing political quagmire

As I stepped outside, wide eyed,
My mother turned her head toward the gate;
There was a soldier's uniform in our yard,
I stood agape in uttermost bewilderment,
A chill ran through my body
And the hair stood up on my head;
I knew for certain that hell was imminent.

Rumour had had it, we harboured terrorists at night!
A malicious rumour echoed by paid informers,
Goodie-goodies who had no soul, no heart,
Who for self or money could betray their mothers;
The soldier's uniform was heinous ploy,
I reported the case to the police station without delay,
I saved everybody at home from a dreadful day.

DELAYED EQUITABLE LAND DISTRIBUTION

In the fertile land spread the blooming fields,
They were a pride and glory of the nation,
The harvest everywhere overfilled granaries,
Various farm produce, vegetables, fruits, rice, corn
And many more, lay in abundance in food markets,
The commercial farmers provided needed employment,
Most communal farmers were more than self sufficient.

Live stock flourished in the commercial farming zone
And no less better in the communal farming zone,
They both contributed to national food production;
The country was the bread basket of the region,
Meat, milk and other related live stock products
Adequately fed the country's internal markets,
A sizable amount was available for country's exports.

The country today reeks in sordid poverty,
The country's economic backbone has been broken,
Undermining the country's manufacturing industry
To a miserable state of desolation and destruction-
Some mines, factories, large and small went down,
Others fled to other countries to escape economic ruin
Due to sudden seizure of private farms by indigenous people
For failure of government to provide viable control
Over the dismantling of the land distribution structure
That was created by greed and domination,
That impoverished black people by its racial structure,
They delayed equitable land distribution.

A REFUGEE

Unfortunately, they call me a squatter
Because I am homeless, I am a refugee!
Like them, I have a mother and father,
But my beloved country needs to be free;
Rooted, wide greed in my country rules,
The homeless, the poor now roam the streets
And the rich and powerful guard their riches.

As a foreigner, driven out of my country,
I should mind always where I tread,
Lest I be caught napping and be sorry
When they send me back to my dread;
Their masters' interests must be served,
Nothing is for nothing in this miserable world;
Safe I am if my presence pays some dividend.

Only a refugee knows how hard it is to be a refugee!
Knowing, every morning, I am, perhaps, unwelcome
And my limitations are on the wall, I am never free,
And if the truth be told, I live in the gloom.
I resisted forces of greed, oppression by the regime,
I escaped when they coined me an enemy of the state,
They wanted me to arrest, even on lawful dissent.

A CHAMELEON

The seeds of hate had been sewn,
Intentionally skewed to induce tribal conflict,
For exploitation in fighting perceived opposition,
To establish and consolidate a one party state;
Then, they unleashed brutal sycophants
Who, as if possessed by diabolical spirits,
They descended upon innocent people like wild beasts.

In broad day-light, on murderous spree,
They got off trucks, attacked people waiting for a bus,
Terrified a few people managed to flee,
Others bore the boots, the fists of the soldiers
Who were altogether out of control and vicious,
Bent on brutalising, maiming people at will,
And they were in the mood to shoot to kill.

They knew, crying would come to naught,
Yet they cried and their children cried in terror,
Birds that had sung, chattered nearby became silent
As people's groans, screams echoed in the forest,
Then, one of the soldiers killed a reptile at his feet,
They coerced one woman to eat the reptile,
And she ate the chameleon, terrified for her life,
Her stomach heaved the dread meet to expel,
But out of terrible fear she couldn't vomit the foul reptile;
Their hearts were made of stone
As to render such horrific torture and malice
Upon a defenceless woman while her small child,
In her arms, haplessly twitched and screamed.

SUCCESS WAS AT HAND

When the plane touched down at the airport,
There it was! I saw it parked at the airport,
The plane high-jacked in mid-air on its direct flight,
With contract workers for neighbouring country's mine,
By freedom fighters to a new destination;
They parked it at the airport, in the open-
It was a testimony of the power of the revolution.

There it was! I saw the testimony laid bare,
At the airport, paraded,
What I had heard before was not a rumour
But a fact that hit the enemy's heart hard,
The high-jacking could, by others be condemned
But, then, I felt a surge of hope, I was elated,
The inevitable war was on, success was at hand.

The sun had moved passed mid day,
When tired, determined faces that filled the plane,
Alighted, were received at the passenger bay
By freedom fighters, as it later became known
And without civilities were led into waiting trucks;
As if an enemy was larking, we were whisked away
In army trucks through a bush road on our way;
I had set myself on a dangerous mission
And I believed I had made the right decision.

I thought then, there was no looking back,
As I saw anxious faces around me that seemed withdrawn,
I realised then, they would look after my back,
And I was delighted we were in it together;
And our lives depended on each other.

HOPE

There is no hope in site at the end of tunnel,
Everything appears gloomy and unattainable,
Dejection, desolation and despair
Abound and roam in the sultry air;
But I cannot give up, as long as I live,
All my goals I have set myself to achieve;
Any difficulties might stand on the way,
They will be just part of the fray,
They cannot deter me completely,
No matter their magnitude and complexity,
Because I have more to lose by giving up,
I will stick always to my everlasting hope.

It would be suicidal to surrender to failure,
Let alone, in this cruel, miserable world, where
Men's machinations are beget of covet
And greed and insatiable appetite
For mammon and absolute power
That perpetuates existence of the poor;
I sought knowledge and advice from the educated
Who claim to be wise and learned,
But success still remained elusive,
For I lacked proper connections to survive;
Then, I conferred with my closest colleagues,
They said, like them, I needed perseverance;
I knelt down on mother earth to beg my ancestor
For help so that I succeed in my endeavour,
Again and again and again to no avail,
Then, I looked up to heaven, prayed sincerely
To Almighty God for his help, for His mercy,
My belief and faith in God gave me hope and peace.

COMERCIAL FARMS

The commercial farms, form the wonderland
The most flourishing expansive private land,
Owned by the local elite and by foreigners-
Exclusively, descendants of colonists,
By few indigenous people as window-dressers
And by local and foreign corporations,
But, note unfair distribution of land to the people,
It was instituted during the ugly days of colonial rule.

Private commercial farms in the country
That contributed to the country's vibrant economy,
Were, plausibly, seen as bread-basket of the region
By foreign economists and economists within,
Have, by nature of their existence, vanished into oblivion
In the most pathetic and destructive fashion,
A legacy of inequity and greed by colonists
That led to private famers, farm employees,
To be brutally assaulted by the marginalised populace,
They were led by ex-combatants to occupy farms by force.

Some farmers, abruptly fled the country,
Having sold some of their property,
Others tried to fight their cause in courts in vain;
Farmers were partly to blame for the confrontation,
They tarried, unwilling to share the land,
Until indigenous people, hitherto marginalised,
Settled in the commercial farms by force,
And the status quo succumbed to new settlers' stance.

Without the necessary farm equipment,
Incompetent in commercial farm management,
The hungry for land indigenous people
Occupied the private farms by force, at will,
The private farms were dealt a fatal blow,
The bread basket of the region was no more,
Because the new settlers had no capital base;
The government, in limbo, didn't give assistance,

Then, continued chaos and lawlessness.
Tribalism tainted the new land distribution exercise,
Setting a stage for racial, regional, tribal squabbles,
That was recipe for confrontation for future generations.

DESPARATE MEASURES

The whole country was paddling through hard times,
In a political deluge that ruined many homes,
Men were picked up, without trial, sent to prison,
They were the regime's desperate measures,
Men, women, children were tortured for information
On the where about of some terrorist,
They took away their livestock as punishment,
They were accused of assisting some terrorist.

The plight of desperate children in a village or town,
Made normal minds recoil;
Most youth roamed the streets, unemployed, forlorn,
Some with certificates from college or school,
In a country so rich in natural resources,
But robbed from without, within and without recess,
Consequently many fled to beef the war, as an option.

The oppressive regime had sunk so low
In its bid to hold to power by any means possible,
They used even ways tested by their forefathers before,
Instead, all their effort inflamed the black people,
The power of majority people grew faster than before;
The ascendance of a black government looked more certain,
It dismayed the regime and the imperial domain.

POVERTY

Poverty, you are a scourge in human existence,
You reduce many people to subhuman,
And you have led some people to hopelessness,
Self denial and oftentimes to suicide,
You are the worst enemy of every soul,
And you rent every soft heart, every loving home,
And you are the product of selfishness and greed-
The horrific sources of all grinding evil,
And exploitation of man, the use of man as capital
From which you grow and multiply,
To torment innocent souls as they labour to supply
The privileged with your cheap labour for their capital,
To serve, forever, their insatiable desire for wealth,
Whereas equity, justice, reason, less prevail.

They would rather call you less privileged
Than call you poor, lest they be ashamed,
People's level of performance is in degrees by nature
But poverty, in essence, cannot be the measure;
The less privileged people are the marginalised,
And their rights are, by system design, curtailed.

THE DREADFUL RUMOUR

The chickens gathered as they picked fallen corn
Around a large, smooth grinding stone,
Under a big, tall and green deciduous tree
That stood in the yard at the west end of the fence.
And the sun had risen an hour in the east,
The warm rays welcome to all creatures, man and beast,
The blue sky clear above and down the horizon further,
The weak cool breeze blowing the light humid air,
And birds in the bushes near the village and further
Chattering and singing in the wonderful summer,
As I stood, silent, contemplating, keeping my ears alert;
I held my trembling heart, outside my little hut.

Gloom hung in the summer morning air,
Everything seemed at stand still, then, I remember,
I was overwhelmed by the dreadful rumour
That the regime's agents had me on their hit list,
For harbouring and assisting a terrorist!
A false accusation based upon hateful intentions,
Perhaps, from an informer to get some benefits,
Or I was to be a sacrificial lamb, by secret police's lies,
To induce fear in the village and the location,
But what I knew for certain then,
My only hope to evade the pending doom,
I had, at once, to flee away without returning home.

STREET KID

Many children some less than seven years of age,
Neglected by their parents relatives and society at large,
Roam the streets homeless and destitute and helpless
And dejected and with dishevelled hair and parched lips,
With tired faces, watery eyes and bare unwashed feet,
Famished, begging for money to buy something to eat
Or foraging for castaway food in the smelling rubbish bins;
And some, at their tender age, take solace in taking drugs,
Others fall prey to malicious child labour, sexual abuse,
A scene that ought to touch even the most callous heart,
A sight which honest people may not want to remember,
The sight is so disturbing, inhuman, dire and lamentable;
"Children are a heritage from the Lord", says the Bible.

Every child needs parental guidance, discipline and care,
Every child needs protection and deserves parental love,
Even animals protect their off springs and show some love,
Every child has the inherent right to proper education
And all parents should be source of their children's aspiration
So that every child can become an asset to the nation;
These children have been nicknamed street kids,
Their plight is an ugly product of greed and selfishness,
But people who are the cause for the suffering of children,
On judgement day, shall meet the wrath of God for the sin.

PEACE

I sought, struggled for freedom to attain peace,
I fought for democracy but I never found peace,
Even in countries, hitherto occupied, under oppression
But have fought and successfully expelled domination
And celebrated happily their hard won independence,
The facts on the ground still parade scarcity of peace.

I have heard people talk so much about peace,
While everywhere, frighteningly, glares injustice,
Some people have been acclaimed lovers of peace-
A title, in this miserable world, that raises a question,
How free are those who qualify them? That is the question;
There are people that struggle peacefully for justice,
They are never proclaimed as initiators of peace.

I hear people who claim to be champions for justice
But they use every force available to themselves
To cower other people to submission and silence
And leave behind a trail of destruction, blood and corpses,
Then, they loot and plunder, in their wake, without remorse,
They must fill their insatiable desire for wealth and power.

HE DIDN'T FLINCH

Two hundred metres away the grocery shop stood,
Surrounded by forest and a clear area to the road
That snaked its way for miles and miles from the city,
Through dry prone region to far west of the country
Where sporadic exchange of fierce gun fire often ensued,
Freedom fighters often outwitted the army and vanished,
They never fought an open war-fair in the battlefield.

They watched that nobody escaped from the shop
As their two army trucks approached the slope,
But a lion emerged from the shop ominously,
An apparition! How on earth could he stand so stubbornly?
And he stared at the soldiers as they disembarked,
He stood his ground, as the trucks stopped in the yard,
A few soldiers, rowdy, entered the grocery shop,
A tense atmosphere seemed to control their every step,
Some soldiers positioned themselves in the trucks,
Others went behind the shop and the trucks,
The lion's eyes never let go their every movement,
He didn't flinch when a few bold soldiers went past,
Close to where he stood, into the shop,
Then, he turned and moved back into the shop,
And with a low, grating voice, his piercing eyes
Madly wide and watching the door and every face,
He ordered the shopkeeper to pack his grocery in a box,
He pulled a cigarette with his left hand from his pocket,
While his right hand remained in the other pocket,
One of the soldiers offered him a light,
Then, the freedom fighter grabbed his parcel and left,
His right hand still in his pocket, he entered the road,
And continued steadily, the same pace, looking ahead,
As the road turned he vanished into the forest;
They gave him almost thirty minutes head start,
Then, they drove off in their planned pursuit,
Minutes later the lead trick was blown up into the air
As a loud bang rent the air from a land mine,
Cloud of dust rose toward the blue sky, blinded the sun,

And splinters of metal, pieces of flesh, flew into the air,
The following truck halted in a barrage of gun-fire,
Some soldiers threw away their guns and fled,
Many soldiers, most of them young men, died
From an unnecessary, futile and deadly adventure,
It was initiated by egoistic leaders, driven by greed and power.

AN ANGEL

Before the school's opening day, two o'clock at noon,
Lost at my work, in the classroom, alone,
A slight undecided knock on the window I heard;
Shaken, apprehensive, through the window I peeped;
She stood there smiling, staring with innocent eyes,
I greeted her, she responded with a cheerful voice
That sounded as if we had been friends before,
Perplexed, I asked her to go to the front door,
She said, she was in a hurry to her home then,

When I invited her for dinner, she accepted, off she ran,
I remained wondering, what her intentions were;
She was barely fifteen years old, I was knew to her,
Why did she knock at the back of the building?
Something sinister and dangerous was lacking!
Her untimely visit, perhaps, could be a blessing.

She was at my house, as invited and on time,
She sat opposite me beaming in smiles, at home,
As we chatted at dinner, I felt as if she was my sister;
She talked about herself freely with happy laughter,
She said, with her mother and sister she lived
At their village, five hundred metres from the school yard,
Her father worked in town and visited every month end,
Then, the crunch! She invited me to sleep at her home,
Lost on how to respond I said nothing, I was mum,
Somehow at last, I said, "yes", I had no reason to refuse;
Her eyes brightened with happiness, she left my house.

She was an Engel! Her visit should have given me the clue,
But, as a doubting Tomas, I took no heed, while I knew
That the school was situated in the battle zone,
I was likely to be the target, since I was unknown.

At ten o'clock at night, I and other teachers
Were raided, beaten up with fists by intruders,
Led, in a stampede, to a large classroom,

And ordered to piled books, chairs, into the storeroom
Until the pile reached the ceiling level,
Then, I was ordered to set fire to the pile,
With my mind racing, my fingers shivering, I struggled
To set fire, with a match stick, to the pile;
The headmaster stood as if waiting for his funeral,
Our armed guests stood watching from outside.
It became obvious we would, by fire, be engulfed,
I slowly moved past the headmaster to get out
And the headmaster pathetically followed suite,
As the flames raged and through the roof burst,
The freedom fighters silently disappeared into the night.

SHE WAS DEAD

She creamed until her screams fell into burning sobs,
She screamed again, twisting, pulling her mother's dress,
Climbing over her, calling for her mother's attention;
She was thirsty and hungry and desperate and forlorn.
A chicken with its chicks that had been hunting for food,
Picking ants, grass, anything they could find in the yard,
Had vanished behind the huts, to the far end of the yard,
Below a large lone orange tree where it squatted,
Covered its chicks with its wings and remained silent,
Facing the direction of the creaming child and alert,
And frequently scanning the sky above;
Other chickens and cork took refuge in the chicken run,
They stayed alert, watching for predators on the move.
Birds in the nearby bushes had, altogether, either flown
Away, or on trees, in silence, as if awaiting pending doom;
There was no sound in the huts, yard, bushes, villages,
Except the child' screams that intensified the existing gloom.

In the blue sky, a few grey clouds lazily floated,
The sun peeped down to a world that seemed void,
Motionless bodies lay scattered in the yard,
Corpses of victims from a ruthless army bent on blood,
Which, on its mission in search of dissidents or terrorists,
Deliberately made many innocent people victims;
The child had cried for too long, she fell asleep,
Her feet, dress, hair, face, hands were smeared with blood
From her mother's gushing wound on the head,
And her mother lay still, she was cold, she was dead.

THERE WERE NO BEGGERS

All you the oppressed generation,
You have the cause to mourn today
For you have little knowledge of the past;
The wisdom passed on for generations,
Alas! It has been meticulously demolished;
It was the cornerstone to true humility,
Self realisation, self discipline, self identity,
Self esteem, the justifiable road to man wood,
It enabled a man to earn his proper position
As the protector and the head of the family,
And the ascendance to plausible woman wood
That made the woman the pillar of love,
Respect, strength, hope and joy
For every family, and made home homely;
Poverty was not a curse, no beggars existed,
Nor was poverty the product of the rich,
The rich lent the poor cattle for work and milk,
Gave them a cow yearly for caring live stock;
From child wood you lent, by giving you get grace,
And you shied from greed and selfishness;
There will always be enough for everybody,
The world needs to rid itself of the selfish, the greedy.

Imagine how the nation would be like today,
With the advent of science and technology,
If every child had full access to education,
If greed and selfishness were non-existent,
Indeed, our country would be a heaven on earth;
Groan and mourn you the new generation
For what you have today is false glory, a myth;
The motto is, one for himself and God for us all,
It is a realm where only the fittest survive, the jungle law.

MORAL GUIDENCE

My mother was an angel, caring and full of love
With a beautiful and cheerful face that could relieve
A sad and overburdened heart to smile,
And my father was a man of honour and principle;
Come evening, my sisters, brothers, I and our mother
Would gather to tell stories that raised laughter,
And neighbours' children often came to join the chorus,
And we listened, told stories, made the evening joyous.

Often we sat ourselves around the wood fire,
In front of our mother's hut,
Under a bright moon lit, clear sky,
As our mother, with a serene face,
Related to us some folk stories one after another-
Some fiery tales that made us flinch,
And made our hairs stand on our heads,
Others were beautiful love stories,
Others were funny stories that left us awash with tears,
But all the stories had moral guidance in our lives.

I LIKED HERDING MY SHEEP

I enjoyed herding sheep always alone,
With nothing to worry about under the sun,
And enjoyed my day with nature in freedom,
Where a field once stood close to my home-
The discarded field, dotted with trees and shrubs,
And endowed with evergreen and plentiful grass,
Where previously thrived millet and ground nuts
On the north, east, west our field was bounded
By a thick forest with undergrowth intertwined,
While toward my home the horizon was far below,
And my home lay just about a stone throw.

I admired my sheep grazing in the area,
Where neither fetid nor sultry was the air,
And admired the lambs, healthy, agile and beautiful,
As they frisked up and down in rare style,
In a graceful and lovely manner, as if in competition,
The morning was often cool with a lovely sunshine.
I marvelled at a lamb sucking from its mother,
The lamb danced its tail in perfect pleasure.

All around birds chirped, chattered far and near,
In various tones and tunes sensational to hear,
And I listened amused, in pleasing wonder,
To birds' melodious songs here and there,
But I quietly retreated in fear,
When I saw an owl on a tree branch near,
Since I had heard before, suspicious stories,
Owls were night agents for witches.

I observed different types of butterflies
As they hovered about beautiful flowers,
Their bright spotted wings vertical to the sky
As if in a show of pride and majesty,
They revealed attractive, magnificent colours,
Whenever they perched or rested on a flower
Or leaf or anywhere for that matter,

75

In search of food from different flowers,
Or to lay their eggs on leaves,
Or perhaps in search of mating partners,
Or perhaps to hide from predators flying above,
Their colourful wings couldn't be seen from above.
Others butterflies with dark coloured wings
Held their wings low as cover,
As if they were in hiding from predators.

 I collected clay at a little dam,
Close to where often I grazed my sheep,
And I moulded toys that depicted my home.
And made toys of elephants, cows and sheep,
And I would let them dry up in the sun,
Then, I would heave a sigh of complete satisfaction.
 .
Under the deciduous tree I squatted
And passersby could hear the cracking sound-
Dux-dux-dux, with handy granite stones,
As I cracked open the "marula" nut shells,
They were big, palatable and delicious,
And I ate the delicious nuts in perfect bliss,
In my small, perfect world without a hiss.

All around, nature seemed in perfect harmony,
And lively and full of beauty and full of joy,
I had so much to observe and admire,
I had so much to touch in wonder,
I had so much to enjoy and be satisfied,
I liked heading my sheep in our old field in deed.

WATER INFRASTRUCTURE

Outside towns and cities life is a gigantic nightmare!
When the heavens fail to open to deliver needed water
For watering field crops, pastures for domestic animals,
Life becomes difficult to bear for both men and animals
Due to lake of means to hold water from flowing to sea,
But the authorities, it seems, they have no eyes to see,
And oftentimes animals, in their great numbers, perish,
But carnivorous- hyenas, wild dogs, wild cats and vultures
Find easy meal from carcasses and sickly herb eaters.
Sometimes government declares drought affected areas
As areas in need of food assistance or disaster zones;
Dry years of late happen more frequent than in the past,
People survive on benevolent bodies' untimely handout
That often takes, days, weeks, months to be available,
Many die while on the waiting least of the hungry people;
Desperate, some leave village homes in hopeless pursuit
For some work in towns or cities but land on predicament
Of worse magnitude than their previous condition,
While the country's leadership, in their mansions, dine,
A chunk from the disaster fund furnishes their dinner tables
And fatten the pockets of their ever lacking sycophants,
They support the pillars of the privilege class and misrule,
And out of greed, selfishness, the leadership built
Inadequate water infrastructure for its people,
But good rainy seasons were inconsistent.

ANTS

I took a walk to the forest close to where I lived
Just to enjoy the aroma from blooming flowers,
I came across your path, and curious I stopped
To observed you as you hurried on your road,
I followed your road to your nest,
Then, to the opposite direction I tracked your road
Wondering what I would find next;
Your workers thinned out and your road just ended.

Your road was neat and of any obstruction cleared
Right from your hunting territory up to your nest;
I saw you probe your way with feelers, and
You left your road to hunt for food, and returned
To your road by the shortest way without getting lost,
Carrying or dragging food by your vice jaws clenched,
Even food greater than your weight or bigger than you are,
Assistance from other workers was always there.

Your road was always crowded with busy workers,
Some going out, others carrying food to the nest,
I thought a fight would breakout for space,
But the behaviour among workers stayed at its best,
They either assisted each other in carrying the food to the nest,
Or gave each other the way to pass;
I became sad why humility among human beings is so less.

FAITH

Oh faith! How you stand high and invincible,
You are the true foundation of all success;
Light that bright flame, the source of hope,
To awaken good ways that lie in me lifeless,
Strengthen my will power against evil spirits,
Let me lean on you in the name of Almighty,
And let all what I do resonate in harmony.

Faith, come and abide in me in God's name,
Light every chamber in my heart
With your bright perpetual flame,
Which strengthens my belief and blunts all doubt,
And which is a source of love for God the Almighty,
Of hope, love for my neighbour, love for my family
And love for all God's creation including my country.

Darken all the ways of the devil,
Make them as hideous as they truly are,
Block every path with concrete wall,
With barbed steel wire, with woven thorns
And with anything that will render it impassable;
The devil's path belongs to the wicked and covetous,
The faithless who mistake lust for love,
On neighbour's suffering, misfortunes, sweat, they thrive
And whose faith is in money and dominance.

HE IS GONE

Of natural causes her brother has not died,
His death came, in broad day-light, looking at his eyes,
They dealt him a deadly blow with purpose;
And she knows how innocent her brother has been,
That he had long resigned his job as policeman-
The regime's injustice was worse than he could sustain-
And the oppressive regime had set him free;
He has been killed by a ruthless gang on murderous spree.

Now he is gone, his wife's situation is bitter,
His children now are a burden to their mother;
All along she has been a house wife,
From now onwards, they will have abnormal life,
In this crumbling and miserable world,
Their loving father, their bread winner is dead;
The death of her brother left her a suppurating wound.

Oh death! Now look at her, at her pitiful eyes,
Her heart is sunk, her burning tears
Flow down her pale wrinkled chicks;
You have robbed her of her brother
Whom she so loved and looked at as her father,
Now he is gone, his children now have no father;
And seated now by her side is her daughter,
She tries hard to sooth her mother
Who ceaselessly, for her painful loss,
From the wounded, bleeding heart, whips,
Her brother has been murdered.

THE WAR

For too long the burden of colonial injustice,
Perpetrated indiscriminately with utter insolence,
Beyond the realm of a civilized human race,
By the mindless settler regime that pursued
The torture, physically, mentally, per designed
Discriminatory laws and regulations and rules,
Applied upon indigenous population in all places,
In education, employment, and the worst of all,
In land distribution, was hurtful, devastating gall.

Injustice that was directed against black people,
That dealt havoc on black's lives of the rank and file,
Was articulated through the imperial constitution,
Aimed   at   oppressing   the   blacks   into   submission

And designed to consolidate the colonial power
In order to prolong the settler regime's rule forever,
To retard economic progress of black people
So that they remained subservient to the regime's rule,
And designed to monopolise the use of land
In favour of whites who were allocated massive land,
And denied black people right to productive land-
A born of contention for many years that followed.

The black people's dissent was met with brutal force,
But they persisted on the fight for equality and justice,
Some had dogs released upon them, others were beaten
And dragged and thrown into police vehicles or army truck
And without court proceedings were thrown into prison,
Others, fleeing the force's brutality, were shot at the back
And died on the spot or on the way to a nearest hospital,
None could be held accountable!

The settler regime rejected one man one vote,
They were in the minority in a racially contested vote,
Due to a culture it had hitherto happily created and
It declared unilateral independence from its motherland,

Only to invoke inflamed international condemnation,
Greater resistance by black people against oppression,
A relentless and vicious war for independence ensued.

One man one vote was the only route out of impasse,
While anything short meant destruction and loss
Of economic infrastructure, property and human life,
But the wealthy and powerful will support every strive
To obliterate any situation that lessens their superiority,
Since they have capital to rebuild destroyed property,
After all, that is the way they acquired their wealth,
And he who dies fighting on their behalf is given wreath
But others may die, including children, except their kin
Provided security of their wealth, power remain certain.

How painful life can be for a person in his native land,
Whatever opinion one holds, the pain is worse felt
More often than not, by him who bears the wound;
They were discriminated by their government,
Therefore, they had to fight for their freedom,
For equity, their dignity and to set free every home.

The majority people welcomed the call for war,
Regardless of the consequences of the war,
Than to brook the yoke of colonial oppression
That brutally silenced dissent on its mission
To subdue the black people, to prolong colonial rule,
And all what the settler regime did was to no avail.

LAND QUESTION

Land allocation became a painful issue
With the advent of fortune seekers from Europe,
They had hitherto settled in the country to the south,
When they ventured, for their empire, to the north,
In their quest for fortune, uncompromising, ruthless,
Their desire for wealth driving them against all odds,
And their goal set to conquer, to establish colonial rule,
They craftily presented themselves as peaceful people,
Sought permission from the local ruler to mine for gold
And other rare and precious minerals in the land,
But, they were in one hand holding the Bible as Christians,
While in the other armed heavily with lethal weapons
To conquer, subjugate the inhabitants of the country,
And to annex to the South their new subdued territory;
They were, for all purposes, nothing less than wolves,
They wore sheep skins as cover for evil ambitions,
That is, to grab the land and its abundant resources.

The warlike white settlers grabbed the land,
In a fierce battle, left thousands of inhabitants dead;
The blacks pressed forward in large numbers,
And the ground vibrated from their battle cries,
As each faced blazing machine gun, without fear,
While armed with a shield and a short spear,
Thousands never saw again the sun;
Daring, bold and fearless, the country's army perished,
And no soldier was spared to bury the dead.
Many white settlers too, in the battle, lost their lives,
Their servants, their children and their wives;
Decaying corpses lay dejectedly on the earth
That was sodden with blood, fetid stench of death.

For the land they died, in the battle field their spirits lie,
A noble cause for patriotism, for honourable men to die,
And they joined their ancestors to continue the war
Until the white invaders who had become a sore,
The foreigners who had large transparent ears,

The marauding invaders who hid their knees,
Were slaughtered in the country or fled,
Or all the black man would rather be dead.

The black man's army was defeated, routed out,
Their ruler, his army annihilated, sneaked out
Of the scene, vanished forever into the unknown,
He abandoned, at the mercy of invaders, his nation.

The black men were coercively resettled
On poor land, then called designated tribal land,
Less productive, with poor clay and sandy soils,
That was previously inhabited by wild animals.
They were forced to pay tax for their cattle per head
And forced to pay for every dog they owned,
And had to sale their cattle to avoid instant prison,
That was the recipe for irreconcilable situation,
That worsened the ever suppurating land question.

BLIND MISDIRECTED VENGEANCE

In living memory that was a bleak wicked day,
When from nowhere the army, in full combat,
Attacked mercilessly everyone on its way,
In search of dissidents who were nonexistent.

He was sent to buy a loaf of bread
At a shop four kilometres away,
The only nearest shop around,
He was caught in the army's net that day.

The local people whom he found at the shop
Were all under siege, terrified and hapless,
Some with bloody broken teeth, without hope,
Others were drenched in their blood and helpless.

He emerged into the clearing of the shop's yard
Eager to see the cause of tumult he had heard
When he was more than a hundred paces back;
He had stopped, listened, nearly turned back,

He wondered what in the village was so amiss!
And curiosity led him into living hell,
What he witnessed was a dreadful experience,
He could have run away but at his own peril.

A blast into the air with a threatening gun
That sent chill, trauma on every man, woman,
People stampeded with such dreadful speed
Into an army truck, in utmost fear, wide eyed.

They tussled in fear of merciless soldier's boot
Or soldier's swinging, murderous gun but,
 Into an army truck that was already overloaded,
They were unaware, their destination was a graveyard.

He could have run away to save his life,
But he knew he could not outpace the bullet,

Instead, he prayed to God to save his life
Then, a soldier blinded him with the gun butt.

He staggered holding his forehead in one hand
As piercing pain raced through his limping trunk
And he tried in vain to regain his mind
But his strength left him, to his knees he sank.

He heard a desperate cry of a child,
A woman wailing and begging for mercy,
The groaning of a man as he fell to the ground;
All were tortured upon blind misdirected vengeance.

When his head cleared he was being tugged
Into the bush by man armed with guns,
With hard faces, ragged, horrid and wicked,
He faced interrogation about dissidents.

He was only twelve years of age,
Simple, and born of unsophisticated parent,
Living with his grandparents of advanced age
In a poor secluded hamlet far remote.

He had heard people talk about dissidents
But no one had seen them in the location;
Still they cut his stomach, exposing his intestines
Because he cried unable to answer any question.

His intestines, studded with sand, looked filthy
As he pushed them into his belly with his fingers;
And he crawled his way home to safety,
He made his way past fluttering leaves, chattering birds.

While they tormented him, he thought of his home;
Content, they left him unconscious, alone to die
But they will live with the sin until Kingdom come,
And they will be condemned by God to die.

FREEDOM

Oh freedom how cherished but elusive!
So many people labour and in bondage live;
Without you my body is weak, my spirit is low,
Freedom, I seek you, to embrace, to adore,
There is no freedom where there is no peace,
There is no freedom where there is no justice,
Neither can peace exist at all without justice,
But greed and power are enemies of justice.

About freedom and justice I need no lecture,
Nobody is born to toil as a slave by nature,
I resist and reject the cause of ignorance,
But the wicked in subterfuge claim innocence
And preach, so often, highly about democracy
And without shame shine in their hypocrisy.

Misinformation is a scourge, a disease to society,
A rotten lie, a diabolical act that should be excised,
Reporters, devoid of morality, this sin do compound
To meet their master's desire for wealth and power,
Consequently, become accomplices to a loot so bitter
And tarnish the image of an essential profession,
But they claim to represent the interests of the nation.

I wish I could relate freedom to democracy
To explain why people struggle, die for democracy,
Whereas often they find themselves in no man's land,
In a thick jungle where there is no one to give a hand,
Where any form of democracy serves a class of people
Through machinations of some corporate media rule,
They are often under the auspices of the rich and powerful.

How can I have freedom when I am an orphan!
Neither can the child of the poor parent born,
We both have no money to buy education-
An abnormal status as normal citizens of a nation-
Nor can the countless people rendered poor

By the privileged class, by the people in power,
As the greedy people's dogma can proudly tell
Anybody, "Each to himself and God to us all",
That serves well the miser and the powerful,
Dare call themselves free in their miserable existence!
They are content they can vote in their constituency.

As much as I understand from a certain source
There is only one form of a democratic process-
There must be a constitution produced by the people,
The government must be freely elected by the people,
And govern through the express will of the people
And be factually, totally representative of the people-
But the greedy and powerful won't die without a fight
And their influence everywhere will shade light,
While effects of greed, power from without the nation
Are worse than those actually engendered from within,
And if an unfair distribution of national wealth exist,
The majority people belong to the marginalised list.

How can there be freedom when citizens hide
In foreign countries on some political ground,
When so many children, wretched, homeless,
Hapless, helpless and feeding from rubbish bins,
In a country where the jungle law is the norm,
In a country where the innocent is made the victim
Because he opposites the people in power
For treading on the freedom and rights of the poor,
But soon the people shall surmount the misrule,
And freedom, justice, peace shall firmly prevail.

\